Oh My CookBook! Sauce Recipes
for Meat, Poultry, Fish and Vegetables Everyone Loves!

ISBN: 9798573464541

TABLE OF CONTENTS

Desert Sauces

Kitchen Conversions

Spoons & Cups

tsp	tbsp	fl oz	cup	pint	quart	gallon
3	1	1/2	1/16	1/32	-	-
6	2	1	1/8	1/16	1/32	-
12	4	2	1/4	1/8	1/16	-
18	6	3	3/8	-	-	-
24	8	4	1/2	1/4	1/8	1/32
36	12	6	3/4	-	-	-
48	16	8	1	1/2	1/4	1/16
96	32	16	2	1	1/2	1/8
-	64	32	4	2	1	1/4
-	256	128	16	8	4	1

tsp	mL
1/2	2.5
1	5

tbsp	mL
1	15

oz	mL
2	60
4	115
6	150
8	230
10	285
12	340

Cup	mL
1/4	60
1/2	120
2/3	160
3/4	180
1	240

Avocado Sauce for Burger

INGREDIENTS

1 large avocado
(peeled, pitted)
¼ cup plain yogurt
¼ jalapeno pepper
2 cloves of garlic

15-20 cilantro leaves
1 lime
2 tbsp olive oil
a pinch of salt

a pinch of of freshly
ground black pepper
2-4 tbsp water
2 tbsp light cream
(optional)

DIRECTIONS

1. Peel the avocado, remove the pit and cut into cubes.
2. Place the ingredients in a blender bowl. Mix and beat until smooth.
3. Spread the prepared sauce generously over each hamburger bun. Serve the burger with fresh vegetable salad.

Apple Apricot Sauce

Prep Time: 5 mins   **Cook:** 50 mins

INGREDIENTS

1 lb (450 g) apples (sour)   2-3 tbsp butter

1 lb (450 g) apricots   1 cup water

1 onion   sugar, turmeric, cloves

3-4 cloves of garlic   to taste

a pinch of salt

DIRECTIONS

1. Wash the fruit. Peel and core the apples. Remove pits from apricots. Cut into cubes. Put the fruits in a bowl and chop with a blender.

2. Melt butter in a frying pan. Add finely chopped onion. Fry the onion until transparent. Add fruit pulp. Mix well. Add a glass of water.

3. Season with spices and finely chopped garlic, sweeten and salt.

4. Stir occasionally, cook for 18-20 minutes under the lid until thickened. Then it remains only to cool.

5. Sweet and sour and at the same time spicy sauce gives the chicken or turkey a special flavor.

Classic Blue Cheese Sauce

Prep Time: 3 mins   **Cook:** 7 mins

INGREDIENTS

2 oz (50 g) blue cheese

¾ cup whipping cream

DIRECTIONS

1. Warm up the cream in a saucepan. Chop blue cheese and add to the heated cream.
2. Let the cheese melt over low heat, stirring constantly.
3. When the sauce is smooth, turn off the heat and serve hot.

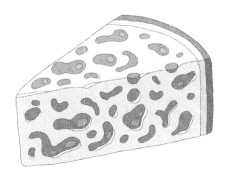

Barbecue Sauce

Prep Time: 5 mins   **Cook:** 10 mins

INGREDIENTS

11 oz (300 g) tomato (ripe)

2 oz (50 g) pitted prunes

1 tbsp sugar

½ oz (10 g) hot pepper

3 cloves of garlic

salt to taste

DIRECTIONS

1. Cut the tomatoes into small pieces and place in a small saucepan. Add sugar, minced garlic and pepper, and finely chopped prunes and heat over medium heat.

2. Bring to a boil, add salt to taste, reduce heat to low and cook for 10 minutes, stirring constantly to prevent the sauce from burning. Chill and serve with grilled meat or kebabs.

Basil Walnut Pesto

INGREDIENTS

2 oz (60 g) basil

2 oz (60 g) chopped walnuts

2 tbsp shredded parmesan cheese

4 tbsp olive oil

1 pinch of salt

2 cloves of garlic

1 tbsp lemon juice

DIRECTIONS

1. Rinse the basil, separate the leaves from the stems and transfer to a mortar. Only the leaves should be used for the sauce, as the stems can give unnecessary bitterness.
2. Cut the garlic into small pieces and place in a mortar.
3. Add walnuts. Pre-grind large pieces with your hands to make it easier to grind the nut.
4. Crush the garlic and basil nuts in a mortar until smooth. Add a pinch of salt.
5. Add the shredded parmesan to the mortar.

6. Add olive oil and lemon juice to the mortar. Use a low intensity oil. Oil that is too intense in taste can simply overwhelm the taste of the basil. Lemon juice is an optional ingredient in pesto, but adds a pleasant sourness to it.

7. Stir the sauce in a mortar until smooth. You can store freshly made pesto in the refrigerator in an airtight jar for 3-4 days.

Bean Sauce

Prep Time: 20 mins   **Cook:** 40 mins

INGREDIENTS

1 tbsp olive oil

1 onion

3 carrots

3 cloves of garlic

4 oz (100 g) lentils

1 lb 5 oz (600 g) peeled tomatoes (canned)

2 tsp curry powder

7 fl oz (200 ml) broth (water)

1 tsp wine vinegar

DIRECTIONS

1. Heat the oil in a saucepan. Peel and chop the onion, wash and chop the carrots. Fry vegetables in olive oil until the onions appear golden brown, add chopped garlic and tomatoes.

2. Rinse lentils, pour into vegetables, stir, add curry, broth and wine vinegar. Simmer for 30–35 minutes until lentils are soft. Cool slightly and beat everything in a blender until smooth.

Beurre Blanc Sauce

Prep Time: 5 mins

Cook: 10 mins

INGREDIENTS

½ onion

4 oz (100 g) butter

5 oz (150 g) white dry wine

dried tarragon (or basil) to taste

DIRECTIONS

1. Chop the onion very finely.
2. Pour wine into a saucepan, add onions. Boil the wine over medium heat, stirring occasionally. The volume of wine should be reduced by 10 times.
3. Divide the butter into 10 pieces. Add butter to the pan one by one, stir. You should make a thick sauce with a sour, onion flavor.
4. Add dried tarragon or basil for an herbal note if desired. The sauce is ready.

Broccoli Cream Sauce

Prep Time: 3 mins   **Cook:** 7 mins

INGREDIENTS

9 oz (250 g) broccoli florets

⅔ cup whipping cream

oil olive (as needed)

3 sprigs parsley

1 clove of garlic

salt and pepper to taste

DIRECTIONS

1. Boil broccoli in salted water in a small saucepan for 5 minutes. Take out and put in a prepared dish.
2. Peel the garlic and chop finely with a knife. Wash and dry the parsley, chop finely.
3. Lightly fry broccoli with parsley and garlic in a frying pan in hot oil, no more than 5 minutes.
4. Add cream and continue simmering for 2 minutes. Season with pepper and salt, stir and remove from heat.
5. Put from the frying pan into a bowl and beat with a blender until smooth.

Cheese Dipping Sauce

Prep Time: 5 mins   **Cook:** 20 mins

INGREDIENTS

5 oz (150 g) camembert cheese

1 tbsp cream cheese

5 tbsp plain yoghurt

salt and pepper to taste

DIRECTIONS

1. Break the camembert cheese into pieces and put in a deep plate, mash with a fork and add cream cheese and yogurt, mix everything well again, salt and pepper. Put in the refrigerator for 20 minutes.
2. If you mix cheeses in a blender, then the sauce becomes more homogeneous.
3. You can add any finely chopped greens to the dip and serve it as a sauce for a steak.

Cherry Sauce

Prep Time: 5 mins   **Cook:** 25 mins

INGREDIENTS

1 lb (500 g) cherries (pitted,

fresh or frozen)

3 whole cloves

1 cinnamon stick

4 oz (100 g) sugar

½ tsp salt

DIRECTIONS

1. Prepare the cherries first. If you are using fresh, then remove the bones, and if frozen, then defrost it a little, put in a saucepan and cover with sugar and salt so that juice appears.
2. Then bring to a boil and simmer for 5 minutes after boiling.
3. Remove cherries from heat and cool slightly. Then beat in a saucepan with a blender until the sauce becomes.
4. Add spices to the chopped cherry - cloves, cinnamon. Boil for 20 minutes to thicken the sauce and saturate the spice.
5. This is an incredibly tasty aromatic and spicy sauce for meat or cheese plate.

Chimichurri Sauce

Prep Time: 5 mins   **Cook:** 5 mins

INGREDIENTS

2 oz (50 g) parsley   2 pinch of salt

2 oz (50 g) tomato   1 tbsp olive oil

½ green hot peppers   1 tbsp vinegar

2 cloves of garlic

DIRECTIONS

1. Rinse the parsley well and cut the stems. We only need the leaves to make the sauce. Chop the parsley coarsely with a knife to make it easier to place in the blender bowl. Peel the garlic, cut the pepper into rings.

2. Put all dry ingredients in a blender bowl, add olive oil and vinegar and beat until smooth.

3. The sauce is ideal for grilled meats and kebabs.

Almond and Wine Sauce

Prep Time: 5 mins   **Cook:** 35 mins

INGREDIENTS

¼ cup almonds

a pinch of ground black pepper

7 fl oz (200 ml) meat broth

2 tbsp white wine

⅓ tsp rosemary

¼ onion

2 tbsp olive oil

1 tbsp flour

DIRECTIONS

1. Add broth, finely chopped onions, white wine, spices and olive oil to a saucepan.
2. Put on fire and bring to a boil.
3. Reduce heat and simmer for half an hour, stirring occasionally with a spoon.
4. To thicken the dish, add a small amount of flour. Cook for a couple more minutes.
5. Meatballs, cutlets with this addition will acquire a unique nutty taste and aroma.

Cocktail Sauce

Prep Time: 5 mins   **Cook:** 5 mins

INGREDIENTS

2 egg yolks

½ cup vegetable oil

1 tsp honey mustard

1 tbsp lemon juice

1-2 tbsp ketchup

1 pinch of black pepper

2 tbsp cognac (or gold rum)

1 pinch of salt

DIRECTIONS

1. Make homemade mayonnaise. In a bowl, combine 2 yolks with a pinch of freshly ground black pepper, 1 tsp honey mustard, 1 tbsp lemon juice and a pinch of salt.
2. Gradually pour the sunflower oil into a bowl, whisking the mixture constantly until thick.
3. Add 1-2 tbsp ketchup to the resulting mayonnaise. You can add a little more or less, be guided by your taste.
4. Then add 2 tbsp cognac and gently stir again with a whisk.
5. The sauce goes well with seafood, fish or salads and snacks.

Creamy Avocado Vinaigrette

Prep Time: 5 mins   **Cook:** 5 mins

INGREDIENTS

1 avocado

4 oz (100 ml) olive oil

2 tbsp lemon juice

1-2 pinches of salt

1 pinch of black ground pepper

1 tsp mustard (optional)

DIRECTIONS

1. Wash the avocado, peel it, cut it in two and remove the pit. Remember to only use ripe fruits that are already soft enough.

2. Place the sliced avocado pieces in a blender bowl and add olive oil. Use olive oil at a low intensity so that the sauce doesn't taste bitter.

3. Add lemon juice, 1-2 pinches of salt and a pinch of ground black pepper. You can also use apple cider vinegar or white wine vinegar instead of lemon juice, which will also taste delicious.

4. Add 1 teaspoon of honey mustard if desired. I tried it with and without mustard, it tastes a little different, but great anyway. Blend the mixture with a blender until a thick, homogeneous mass is obtained.

If you want to make the sauce thinner, increase the amount of olive oil.

5. Serve the sauce with any vegetable salad. It goes well with tomatoes, peppers and cucumbers. Ideal for dressing vegetable salad with shrimps.

6. 6. This dressing will perfectly complement any vegetable salad, and it can also be served with boiled or fried shrimp.

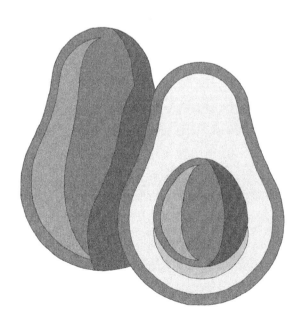

Creamy Silk Sauce

Prep Time: 5 mins   **Cook:** 20 mins

INGREDIENTS

⅓ cup butter

3 tbsp olive oil

4 cloves of garlic

½ onions

¼ cup heavy cream

3-5 sprigs fresh mint

DIRECTIONS

1. Chop onion and garlic finely.
2. In a saucepan, combine butter, olive oil, garlic and onion. Cook, stirring constantly, over medium heat for 15 minutes, until the onions are transparent, but no more. Pour in cream and cook until thickened. Remove from heat.
3. Add freshly chopped mint and beat with a blender on high speed for 10-15 seconds. Cook for another 2-3 minutes with constant stirring. Do not cook for too long as the sauce will begin to break down.

Curd Dipping Sauce

Prep Time: 5 mins   **Cook:** 10 mins

INGREDIENTS

9 oz (250 g) curd cottage cheese

3 tbsp sour cream

3½ fl oz (100 ml) plain kefir (or yogurt)

1 bunch of scallions (green onions)

1 bunch of dill

salt to taste

DIRECTIONS

1. Wash greens, dry and chop finely.
2. Thoroughly grind cottage cheese with salt and mix with kefir, sour cream and herbs, refrigerate for 30 minutes.
3. It is best to use a mortar while stirring for a richer taste. And if you beat the sauce in a blender, then it will become homogeneous.

Eggplant Dip

Prep Time: 5 mins   **Cook:** 35 mins

INGREDIENTS

2 eggplants

3 tbsp olive oil

½ bunch of parsley

2 cloves of garlic

4 tbsp sesame seeds

½ lemon (juice)

salt to taste

DIRECTIONS

1. Grind sesame seeds into a paste with the addition of 1 tbsp olive oil.
2. Wash the eggplants, prick the skin in several places with a fork, grease with oil and bake for 30–35 minutes.
3. Chop the parsley, peel the garlic and chop finely. Mix sesame seed paste with parsley and garlic, add salt and lemon juice.
4. Remove the eggplants from the oven, cut in half, gently remove the pulp with a spoon and mix it with a paste of herbs and sesame seeds. Mix everything thoroughly.

Garlic Butter Sauce

Prep Time: 4 mins **Cook:** 6 mins

INGREDIENTS

5 oz (140 g) butter

3 tbsp lemon juice

5 tbsp garlic powder (or

minced garlic)

2 tbsp grated parmesan

cheese

salt and pepper to taste

DIRECTIONS

1. Melt the butter in a saucepan over low heat. Add the grated parmesan.
2. Season to taste with lemon juice, salt, pepper and garlic.
3. Serve with fish and meat dishes with fresh white bread and salad.

Greek Tzatziki Sauce

Prep Time: 5 mins   **Cook:** 10 mins

INGREDIENTS

(250 g) plain yogurt (thick)   1 clove of garlic

1 bunch of dill   salt and pepper to taste

2 cucumber

½ lemon (juice)

DIRECTIONS

1. Wash the cucumbers, peel and rub on a coarse grater into a bowl. Squeeze the cucumbers out of the liquid, otherwise the sauce will be too liquid, and this is not correct.
2. In a bowl, combine chopped dill, cucumbers, crushed garlic, lemon juice, salt and pepper. Then add yogurt and stir.

Green Sauce

INGREDIENTS

1 bunch of cilantro

a handful of walnuts

2-3 tbsp olive oil

½ lemon (juice)

salt to taste

DIRECTIONS

1. Rinse greens, dry and chop finely.
2. Grind the nuts in a mortar with the addition of 1 tbsp. l. olive- oil and salt.
3. Mix herbs and crushed nuts, pour over the rest of the olive oil and lemon juice.

Harissa Sauce

Prep Time: 5 mins   **Cook:** 5 mins

INGREDIENTS

11 oz (300 g) jalapeno pepper (or other hot pepper)

3 cloves of garlic

4 pinches of ground coriander

3 pinches of ground cumin

3 pinches of salt

1-2 tbsp olive oil

DIRECTIONS

1. Wash and dry the pepper. Cut off the stem, but do not remove the seeds. Cut the peppers into large pieces. Peel the garlic.
2. Place all ingredients in a blender bowl and blend until smooth. Add olive oil and stir. Store the prepared sauce in the refrigerator.

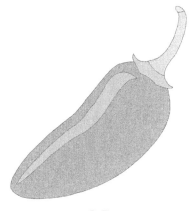

Hollandaise Sauce

Prep Time: 5 mins   **Cook:** 5 mins

INGREDIENTS

3 egg yolks

1 tsp water

1 tbsp lemon juice

2 oz (60 g) butter

1 pinch of salt

DIRECTIONS

1. Pour half a pot of water and bring to a boil, reduce heat to low. In a small bowl, combine the yolks, water, and lemon juice.

2. Place the bowl in a pan. It is important that the bowl is not in contact with the water, but in the steam bath. Whisk the yolks continuously.

3. When the yolks begin to thicken and acquire the consistency of thick sour cream, add small pieces of butter. It should be soft, but a little cold to immediately take the temperature of the sauce onto itself.

4. Cook the sauce for another 1 minute in a water bath, stirring constantly, then remove the bowl from the pan and continue stirring the sauce for another 1 minute, add salt. Serve the sauce warm.

5. Hollandaise goes well with fried or steamed white fish and vegetables and poached eggs.

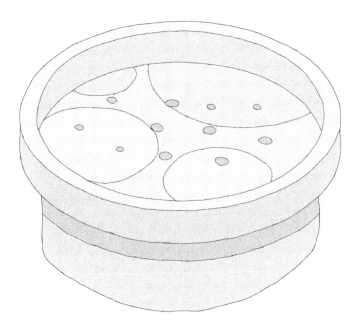

Homemade Ketchup

Prep Time: 15 mins   **Cook:** 60 mins

INGREDIENTS

1 onion

1-2 carrot

2 lb 5 oz (1.5 kg) tomato

2 cloves of garlic

6-7 whole cloves

½ tsp sweet paprika (or smoked paprika)

5 allspice berries

3-4 tbsp vinegar

2 tbsp cornstarch (if you want to thicken the ketchup additionally)

5 tbsp vegetable oil

DIRECTIONS

1. Rinse the tomatoes and squeeze the juice out of them using a juicer.

2. Cut the onion and one carrots into medium cubes. If you wish, you can grate the carrots on a coarse grater. Crush 2 cloves of garlic. Preheat a saucepan with 5 tbsp vegetable oil and fry the onions, garlic and carrots in it over medium heat until the onions are translucent.

3. Add the squeezed tomato juice to the saucepan to the onions and carrots.

4. Then add 6-7 cloves, 5 allspice berries, ½ tsp of sweet or smoked paprika and a few pinches of salt.

28

Simmer the sauce in a saucepan over medium heat for about an hour, or until it has approximately halved in volume. Use a spoon to remove the large allspice peas if desired.

5. Beat the mixture in a blender bowl until a smooth consistency is obtained.

6. Transfer the cooked ketchup back to the saucepan, add 3-4 tbsp vinegar and, if necessary, salt to taste.

7. If you want to further thicken the sauce, you can add 2 tbsp cornstarch, previously diluted in a little cold water.

8. Bring the sauce to a boil and pour into a jar.

Homemade Mayonnaise

Prep Time: 3 mins   **Cook:** 3 mins

INGREDIENTS

2 egg yolks

1 tbsp yellow mustard

1 pinch salt

1 pinch of black ground

pepper

1 tbsp lemon juice

4-5 oz (100-150 ml)

vegetable oil

DIRECTIONS

1. Put 2 egg yolks into a bowl, whisk lightly. Add a pinch of black pepper and salt, a tablespoon of yellow mustard.
2. Then pour in the vegetable oil and mix well with an immersion blender until smooth. The more vegetable oil you use, the denser the texture of the sauce will be.
3. Add lemon juice to the bowl and stir a little more.

Honey Mustard Sauce

Prep Time: 2 mins   **Cook:** 2 mins

INGREDIENTS

12 tbsp mustard

6 tbsp honey

lemon juice to taste

1 small bunch of dill

DIRECTIONS

1. In a small bowl, combine mustard, honey, and finely chopped dill. Season to taste with lemon juice. Serve with fish or seafood.

31

Indian White Sauce

Prep Time: 2 mins   **Cook:** 5 mins

INGREDIENTS

7 oz (200 g) plain yogurt

2 slices pineapple (canned)

½ cucumber

5 sprigs of dill

1 sprig of mint

chili powder to taste

salt to taste

DIRECTIONS

1. Cut pineapple and cucumber into medium cubes.
2. Wash the dill and chop finely.
3. Mix yogurt with pineapple, cucumber, and dill. Stir and season with salt to taste.
4. Add a chopped sprig of mint for freshness.
5. If you like a savory taste, add chili to taste.

Lemon Parsley Sauce

Prep Time: 4 mins   **Cook:** 6 mins

INGREDIENTS

5 oz (140 g) butter

3 lemons (zest and juice)

1 bunch of fresh parsley, chopped

salt and pepper to taste

DIRECTIONS

1. Rub the zest of three lemons and squeeze out the juice. Chop the parsley finely.
2. Melt the butter in a small saucepan. Add lemon juice and zest, cook over low heat for 1 minute.
3. Add the parsley and cook for another 30 seconds. Season to taste with salt and pepper. Stir.

Marseille Sauce

Prep Time: 2 mins   **Cook:** 6 mins

INGREDIENTS

¼ cup butter

1 tsp olive oil

1 pinch of salt

1 pinch dried rosemary

4-6 sage leaves

1 tsp chopped garlic

DIRECTIONS

1. Place butter and olive oil in a skillet over medium heat.
2. When the butter is half melted, add the sage, rosemary, salt and garlic.
3. When the butter has completely melted and begins to crackle, wait a little for the sauce to smell. It will take about a minute.
4. Pour the sauce into a saucepan and serve.

Mushroom Sauce

INGREDIENTS

7 oz (200 g) mushrooms

2-3 tbsp olive oil

3½ fl oz (100 ml) whipping

cream

1 stalk of leeks (white part)

salt and ground black

pepper to taste

DIRECTIONS

1. Cut the mushrooms into slices, cut the leeks into rings and fry them in olive oil until soft.
2. Heat the cream, but do not boil.
3. Remove mushrooms and onions from heat, allow to cool slightly, put in a blender, season with salt, pepper, add cream and beat everything until smooth.

Nacho Cheese Sauce

Prep Time: 3 mins   **Cook:** 7 mins

INGREDIENTS

2 tbsp butter

2 tbsp wheat flour

1 cup whole milk

6 oz (170 g) cheddar cheese

a pinch of salt

¼ tsp chili powder

DIRECTIONS

1. Place the butter and flour in a saucepan over low heat, heat and beat the ingredients into a homogeneous, frothy mixture. Continue whisking for 1 minute.

2. Pour milk into flour and butter mixture. Increase the heat slightly and let the milk warm up while whisking.

3. When boiling, the mass will thicken, as soon as it becomes thick enough not to drip from the spoon, it can be removed from the stove.

4. Pour the grated cheddar cheese into the mass in small portions, stirring constantly.

If necessary, the saucepan can be placed over low heat to allow the cheese to melt completely. The main thing at this stage is not to overheat the resulting cheese sauce.

5. Once the cheese is melted, add chili powder, salt. Too thick mass can be diluted with a little milk.

Peanut Sauce

INGREDIENTS

4 oz (100 g) roasted salted peanuts

2 tbsp honey

1 tsp wine vinegar (or rice vinegar)

8-10 tbsp vegetarian oil

¼ cup water

2-3 tbsp lemon juice

DIRECTIONS

1. Grind peanuts in a blender bowl, add honey, lemon juice, wine or rice vinegar and vegetable oil. The mixture is quite thick.
2. Transfer to a deep bowl and blend with a hand blender. It allows for better chopping and more homogeneity.
3. Start adding water in small portions, adjust the thickness of the sauce as you like. I recommend the consistency of light sour cream.

Pomegranate Sauce

Prep Time: 3 mins   **Cook:** 7 mins

INGREDIENTS

½ tsp dried basil

½ cup semi-sweet red wine

½ cup pomegranate juice

⅔ tsp cornstarch

2 pinch of ground black pepper

1 tsp sugar

½ tsp salt

DIRECTIONS

1. Pour pomegranate juice into a small bowl and add ¼ cup wine. Add salt, sugar, chopped garlic, basil, black pepper.
2. Pour into a saucepan and put on medium heat, let the sauce boil.
3. Dilute the starch in the remaining wine. When the sauce has already boiled, reduce the heat to low and pour the starch into the saucepan, stirring continuously.
4. Heat the sauce, stirring constantly, for about 30 seconds and remove from heat.
5. Serve with meat and fish.

Pumpkin Sauce

Prep Time: 20 mins   **Cook:** 25 mins

INGREDIENTS

14 oz (400 g) peeled
pumpkin

1 fresh hot pepper

1 bunch of cilantro

1 tsp caraway seeds

2 tbsp olive oil

salt to taste

DIRECTIONS

1. Finely chop the pepper (you can crush it in a mortar with the addition of 1 tbsp vegetable oil).

2. Cut the pumpkin into medium cubes, add warm boiled water and salt.

3. Add pepper and put on fire, let the water boil and reduce heat, simmer over low heat for 15 minutes. Rub the boiled pumpkin through a sieve.

4. Wash the cilantro, drain and chop finely, add to the pumpkin puree, pour over with olive oil, add the caraway seeds and mix well.

Quick and Easy Bechamel

Prep Time: 3 mins   **Cook:** 7 mins

INGREDIENTS

2 oz (50 g) butter

2 tbsp wheat flour

1 pinch of ground nutmeg

2 cup whole milk

DIRECTIONS

1. In a saucepan, melt the butter over low heat. It is important that it does not burn.
2. Add wheat flour and stir in butter using a spoon or whisk.
3. Brown for 1-1.5 minutes, until the flour is golden brown.
4. Pour in 2 cups of milk at once and stir constantly with a whisk so that no lumps form.
5. Add a pinch of ground nutmeg and cook until the sauce thickens. It is not recommended to overcook the sauce, it takes no more than 2 minutes to thicken. Serve hot. If the sauce remains, then you can put it in the refrigerator and reheat it with the addition of a small amount of milk.

Store ready-made sauce for no more than 2 days in the refrigerator.

6. This sauce ideally complements steamed or oven-cooked vegetable and fish dishes. And if you decide to make a potato or cauliflower casserole, you can add this sauce to make it even more delicious.

Sauce Gribiche

INGREDIENTS

1 egg yolk

1 tbsp mustard

4-5 oz (100-150 ml)

vegetable oil

1 tsp wine vinegar

1 tbsp capers

2 oz (20-30 g) gherkins

pickles

5 sprigs of thyme

salt and pepper to taste

DIRECTIONS

1. Combine the yolk and mustard in a bowl. Whisk until smooth. Start adding the oil in small portions and continue whisking the sauce. The consistency should be fairly thick.
2. Finely chop the capers, gherkins and thyme. Add salt, pepper and vinegar, chopped herbs, capers and gherkins to the sauce. Stir the sauce well.
3. Sauce is usually served with boiled chicken or fish, and it also ideally complements meat pates.

Spicy Avocado Sauce

Prep Time: 3 mins   **Cook:** 2 mins

INGREDIENTS

2 large ripe avocados

4-6 jalapeno peppers

(depending on desired level

of spiciness)

1 small white onion

2 cloves of garlic

⅓ cup chopped cilantro

2 limes (juice)

4 tbsp vinegar

salt and pepper to taste

DIRECTIONS

1. Peel the avocado and remove the pit. Remove seeds from jalapeno peppers and chop as desired. Peel and chop white onions.
2. Place all ingredients in a blender bowl and blend until smooth and creamy, adjust the amount of spices if necessary.

Spicy Tahini Sauce

Prep Time: 10 mins   **Cook:** 10 mins

INGREDIENTS

3 cloves of garlic   1 green hot pepper

5 tbsp sesame seed   2 tbsp olive oil

½ lemon (juice)   salt to taste

1 bunch of parsley

DIRECTIONS

1. Grind sesame seeds in a mortar to a paste (tahini).
2. Wash the parsley, dry it and chop finely. Chop or crush the garlic in a mortar.
3. Finely chop the pepper.
4. Put all ingredients (except olive oil) in a blender and beat until smooth.
5. Pour olive oil over the sauce before serving.

Tahini Sauce

Prep Time: 5 mins   **Cook:** 10 mins

INGREDIENTS

5 tbsp sesame seeds

6 tbsp plain yogurt (or kefir)

3 tbsp lemon juice

3 cloves of garlic

1 bunch of cilantro

salt and ground pepper to taste

DIRECTIONS

1. Grind sesame seeds in a mortar to a paste (tahini).
2. Wash cilantro, dry and chop finely. Chop or crush the garlic in a mortar.
3. Mix yogurt or kefir with sesame paste, add lemon juice, garlic, chopped herbs, salt and pepper and mix everything well.
4. Store in the refrigerator for no more than a day.

Tartar Sauce

Prep Time: 4 mins   **Cook:** 2 mins

INGREDIENTS

9 tbsp mayonnaise

1 cucumber

2 hard-boiled eggs

3 tsp chopped dill

salt and pepper to taste

2 tbsp capers (can be

replaced with pickled

cucumbers)

3 tbsp whole grain mustard

DIRECTIONS

1. Dice fresh cucumber and eggs. Finely chop the capers and dill.
2. Mix all ingredients. Season to taste with salt and pepper. Stir well and serve with fish and seafood.

Tomato and Apple Sauce

Prep Time: 10 mins   **Cook:** 20 mins

INGREDIENTS

9 oz (250 g) green apples

(sweet and sour taste)

9 oz (250 g) tomatoes

5 oz (150 g) sugar

⅔ cup light cream

salt and pepper to taste

DIRECTIONS

1. Wash the apples, peel and core and cut into small cubes. Cut the tomatoes in the same way.

2. Place apples and tomatoes in a small saucepan, cook over medium heat, add sugar, stir and bring to a boil

3. Reduce heat to low and simmer for 10 minutes. Add light cream and cook for another 5 minutes. At the end of cooking, add salt and pepper to taste.

4. A very simple and tasty creamy sauce and goes well with meat and poultry.

Tuscan Sauce

Prep Time: 10 mins   **Cook:** 35 mins

INGREDIENTS

1 lb (450 g) peeled tomatoes (canned)

1 stalk of leeks (white part)

2 cloves of garlic

1 carrot

1 onion

3½ fl oz (100 ml) olive oil

3½ fl oz (100 ml) of water

1 tbsp sugar

1 sprig of rosemary

1 sprig of basil

salt and ground black pepper to taste

DIRECTIONS

1. Wash the carrots, peel the garlic and onion. Chop the vegetables. Wash the leeks and cut into rings.

2. Heat olive oil in a saucepan, add chopped vegetables, basil and rosemary, fry for 1-2 minutes, add tomatoes, season with salt, pepper, add sugar, mix everything well.

3. Pour in water and cook over low heat for about 30 minutes.

Vegetable Demi-Glace Sauce

Prep Time: 15 mins   **Cook:** 70 mins

INGREDIENTS

¼ celery

1 carrot

1 beet

2 cloves of garlic

5 oz (150 g) green cabbage

1 tbsp ketchup (or tomato juice)

DIRECTIONS

1. Wash celery, carrots, beets and cabbage, peel, finely chop. Add one tablespoon of tomato juice or ketchup. Place in a deep baking dish and stir. Put in the oven for 45-60 minutes and bake at 360°F (180°C). When the vegetables are almost done, add the garlic clove.

2. After 20 minutes, add water to the vegetables in the oven so that it completely covers them.

3. Repeat this step as necessary as long as the vegetables are stewing.

4. Strain the prepared sauce. You should get a rich vegetable mixture that will perfectly enhance the taste of absolutely any dish.

Wine Sauce

INGREDIENTS

3 tbsp butter

2 cloves of garlic

½ shallot

1 tsp dried tarragon

¼ tsp salt

¼ tsp ground white pepper

¼ cup white wine

1 lemon (juice)

1 tbsp fresh parsley

DIRECTIONS

1. Chop the garlic and shallots.
2. Melt butter in a small saucepan over medium heat. Add the garlic and shallots and cook, stirring until the onions are translucent (about 3 minutes). Sprinkle it with tarragon, salt and white pepper.
3. Raise heat to medium and add white wine and lemon juice. Bring to a boil, then whisk for 1 minute. Remove from heat and sprinkle with chopped parsley.

Dessert Sauces

Blueberry Sauce

INGREDIENTS

7 oz (200 g) blueberries

4 tbsp sugar

½ lemon (juice)

3 tbsp plain yogurt

DIRECTIONS

1. Rinse and dry blueberries. Puree all ingredients (except yogurt) in a blender. Add yogurt to the resulting mass and mix well until smooth.
2. If desired, you can take a little more sugar, and less lemon juice. Then the sauce will be sweeter.

Caramel Sauce

Prep Time: 2 mins   **Cook:** 10 mins

INGREDIENTS

4 oz (100 g) powdered sugar

2 oz (50 g) butter

10 fl oz (300 ml) whipping cream

DIRECTIONS

1. Melt the butter in a saucepan and add the powdered sugar, put on fire and heat, stirring occasionally, until golden brown. Add cream and continue heating while stirring. The sauce should thicken slightly and acquire a golden hue. Serve warm.

Chocolate Sauce

Prep Time: 2 mins **Cook:** 10 mins

INGREDIENTS

4 oz (120 g) chocolate

4 tbsp water

4 tbsp whipping cream

1 tbsp powdered sugar

3 tbsp butter

DIRECTIONS

1. Break the chocolate into pieces and melt in a water bath with the addition of powdered sugar, water and half the volume of cream. Once the chocolate is completely melted, remove from heat.
2. Heat the remaining cream (do not boil) and pour into the chocolate, mix everything well.
3. Pieces of butter and add to the base mass, mix well again.

Lemon Sauce

INGREDIENTS

7 oz (200 g) powdered sugar

3 tbsp lemon juice

2 tbsp hot water

DIRECTIONS

1. Sift the powdered sugar through a sieve. Combine lemon juice with powdered sugar, add water and mix everything thoroughly until you get a thick white mass.

2. If you mix lemon juice with lime juice, then the taste of the sauce will become more interesting.

56

Raspberry Mint Sauce

Prep Time: 2 mins   **Cook:** 7 mins

INGREDIENTS

4 oz (100 g) fresh raspberries

1 bunch of mint

4 tbsp powdered sugar

DIRECTIONS

1. Wash the mint, let the water drain and chop finely. Mix raspberries with powdered sugar and rub through a sieve. Mix the resulting puree with mint.

2. You can use a mortar to gradually grind the ingredients. This will make the texture more interesting.

Strawberry Dip

Prep Time: 2 mins   **Cook:** 5 mins

INGREDIENTS

4 oz (100 g) strawberries

9 oz (250 g) cream cheese

3 tbsp powdered sugar

1 tbsp vanilla liqueur

DIRECTIONS

1. Wash the strawberries, remove the stalks. In a blender, puree the strawberries with soft cheese until smooth. Add powdered sugar and vanilla liqueur, mix well together. Put in the refrigerator for 20 minutes.

Vanilla Chocolate Sauce

Prep Time: 2 mins   **Cook:** 15 mins

INGREDIENTS

2½ oz (70 g) dark chocolate

1 oz (30 g) butter

1 tbsp starch

3 tbsp sugar

1 tsp vanilla sugar

7 fl oz (200 ml) water

DIRECTIONS

1. Break the chocolate into pieces, put in a saucepan, add 3½ fl oz (100 ml) of water and heat in a water bath until the chocolate is completely dissolved.

2. Dissolve starch in 3½ fl oz (100 ml) of water, put on fire and bring to a boil, remove from heat. Add starch, sugar, vanilla sugar to the chocolate and heat everything again in a water bath for about 1 minute, stirring constantly.

Printed in Great Britain
by Amazon